P9-CKL-865

BIOTECHNOLOGY
PUBLIC POLICY AND THE SOCIAL SCIENCES
CRITICAL NEEDS IN TEACHING AND RESEARCH

A report to the
Institute for Advanced Study
Indiana University

by

Robert H. Blank
Lynton K. Caldwell
Thomas C. Wiegele
Raymond A. Zilinskas

Bloomington, Indiana 47405

April 1987

ACKNOWLEDGEMENTS

This report was produced while the co-authors served as Fellows of the Institute for Advanced Study of Indiana University during the fall of 1986. We are appreciative of the Governing Board of the Institute for giving us the opportunity to come together to reflect on and write about a matter of urgent national concern. We are also grateful to Dr. Morton Lowengrub, Director of the Institute, Associate Director Albert Wertheim, and Ms. Ivona Hedin, Assistant to the Director, for the many courtesies shown to us during our stay in Bloomington. Mrs. Joan Rillo very cheerfully and accurately typed the report and saw it through numerous corrections and drafts. Patricia Finn-Morris carefully edited the entire manuscript. Finally, we thank our informal reviewers, Dr. Elof Carlson, Dr. Leonard J. Guarraia, and Dr. John Woodcock, who read the manuscript and offered comments. Their insights have greatly strengthened the final product.

The findings and opinions expressed in this report are, of course, those of its authors, and are not to be taken as endorsed either by the Institute for Advanced Study or by the administration of Indiana University.

TABLE OF CONTENTS

I. INTRODUCTION

Science-based biotechnology* is now introducing fundamental changes in the status of life on earth which have major implications for human society, yet the social sciences are largely failing to address these changes. Biotechnology offers immense opportunities for advancing the quality of human life, holding promise for overcoming numerous and heretofore intractable causes of suffering and impoverishment. Moreover, it may enable mankind to enjoy the benefits of science without degradation of the biosphere. But to obtain these advantages, biotechnology must be guided by wise and timely public policies. Even the most beneficent innovation may create problems that, unless anticipated and prevented, may offset or cancel out social gains.

While the natural sciences and humanities have important roles to play in developing adequate responses to questions raised by rapidly advancing technoscience, this report speaks to the social sciences in general and political science in particular. Biotechnology could substantially alter life on earth as we know it, and the policy sciences can no longer afford to neglect this critical area. Of all the advancing technologies, the life sciences and their applications have the greatest portent for our future.

There are risks associated with the new biotechnology, along with widespread disagreements over which of the risks are real and which

---

*See Glossary, page 52, for definitions of technical terms.

imaginary. Moreover, advances in biotechnology enter into aspects of human life and values previously regarded as private or sacrosanct. Few areas of society or the economy, from bedroom to boardroom, will be untouched by new life science findings and applications. Simultaneously, modern society is being drawn into the era of biotechnology with no more than a minimal concern for its consequences and implications. The sensitive and pervasive nature of the issues raised has caused social concern, and has lead to some political response; but this response has been fragmentary, inconsistent, and often polemical. Few criteria or general principles have emerged to guide the course of policy. Modern society finds itself in a major cultural and scientific revolution which it scarcely comprehends and for which it lacks the conceptual and institutional basis for rational policy making.

In the interest of society, the sociopolitical implications of the new biotechnology should receive attention as policy issues commensurate with their far-reaching impacts upon the social order and its individual members. To prepare society to act constructively on matters raised by the new biotechnology, new initiatives in issue-oriented policy research, teaching, and public information are needed. To develop this understanding is a task of education, especially of higher education in our colleges and universities. With few exceptions, this responsibility has not yet been satisfactorily addressed. It is our belief that the rational, safe, and effective utilization of the new biotechnology requires early action by faculties, trustees, presidents, and deans, as well as by private and public institutions whose funding decisions influence directions and priorities in teaching and research.

To establish effective programs of study in public policy for biotechnology will require leadership, conviction, and resources. There are formidable obstacles to the development of such policy studies, foremost being their interdisciplinary character. Serious attention to biotechnological policy will require a reordering of academic priorities and a reconstituting of disciplinary structures. Institutional relationships will need clarification where policy studies have been organized as independent fields of inquiry. Thus a large number of academic disciplines will be affected, especially the social sciences.

Our particular focus is on political science because of its special concern with the forces and processes that generate public policies. In human society there is no escape from politics. But the range and power of the new biotechnology makes imperative a more informed and rational politics. The power of genes, cells, and microorganisms is no less awesome than the power of atoms, and may be more problematic because it is less perceived. Hope for benefits tends to obscure perception of problems and possible hazards. Given the complexities of the biological revolution and its potential advantages for all society, consideration of emerging issues cannot be left solely to polemical and ideological argumentation. It follows that there is a need to develop an academic program and structure bringing all involved disciplines into a harmonious and productive relationship. The task will be difficult, but with resolve and resources it can be done.

This report identifies policy issues arising from biotechnology, advances reasons for their neglect in higher education, and suggests action to remedy this dereliction. The body of the report is divided into five sections. In Section II we describe some of the general social and political implications of an expanding biotechnology. Section III focuses on several specific social and political issues and provides examples of areas in which political scientists could contribute significantly to resolving social problems associated with developments in biotechnology. In Section IV we discuss the broad dimensions of the problem of effecting curricular change in higher education and, in particular, the discipline of political science. Section V describes specific ways in which academic units, private foundations, and government can assist in developing a public policy analysis capability in the United States. Section VI is a concluding summary.

II. IMPLICATIONS OF EXPANDING BIOTECHNOLOGY

The recent advances in the life sciences are often referred to as the "biological revolution."[1] In fact, the phenomenal growth of biological knowledge and technique is more accurately described as evolutionary, with progressive expansion punctuated by spectacular explosions such as the Watson-Crick identification of the double helix, and the development of the technology for recombining DNA. Since the publication in 1854 of Charles Darwin's The Origin of the Species, a series of major advances in biology have led to social and political controversy and changed prevailing beliefs and behaviors. During the past quarter-century these advances have accelerated and expanded on an unprecedented scale. Their effects are now being felt throughout the world.

To further complicate a complex development, the "revolution" in biology is but one of three technological advances promising major changes by the twenty-first century; the others are microelectronics/communications and new materials. Each of these is in an exponential phase of growth, although microelectronics has perhaps a ten-year head start on the other two.

Many of the impacts that these three sets of technologies pose for society are comparable. For example, each has the potential for inducing major changes in life styles and expectations, in some instances approaching "future shock"; and with their deployment, the technology gap between the high technology nations and the Third World is likely to widen. Each could be used by the military for augmenting present weaponry, adding new dimensions to their use, or creating entirely new weapons systems. Nations possessing these technologies are likely to question whether access to them by others should be permitted, especially if there is a prospect of their abusive or hostile use. Not the least, each technology requires for its service many persons possessing multi-disciplinary skills; these capabilities may not be attainable in countries whose facilities for research and teaching are compartmentalized by rigid disciplinary divisions. The responses of universities to the challenges of these far-reaching technological innovations may determine the futures of nations.

Although all three advancing technologies will have significant effects on social issues, the sensitive and unprecedented character of biotechnology will pose the more difficult policy problems[2]. These characteristics are less pronounced in the two other innovating technologies; the developments taking place in them are, in effect, extensions of present technologies. For example, as semi-conductors/communications advance, present computational power will increase and will become available at a lower cost; communications will become easier, faster, less costly, and more pervasive. As new synthetic materials replace natural materials, possibilities for materials usage in industry and commerce will be expanded. As an example, fibre optics will increasingly replace metal transmission lines, thereby increasing the carrying capacity of communications systems, and slowing depletion of non-renewable resources. Important as these and comparable developments are, they will not confront society with unprecedented issues. Biotechnology, however, will.

Evolution or revolution, the phenomenal growth of biology has had two social effects. The first has been conceptual. Darwinian hypotheses in the nineteenth century and genetic findings in the twentieth have caused changes in mankind's self-image. Further, biospheric and ecosystems concepts are altering basic modern assumptions about the relationship of man to nature. But these changing perceptions have not occurred uniformly throughout society. Traditional beliefs coexist with new perceptions. Biotechnologies are not uniformly accepted or regarded as good. Fears--realistic and exaggerated--have been aroused by particular biotechniques (cloning or artificial twinning, for example). During the initial public debate over recombinant DNA (rDNA) there were alarms about the "Frankenstein effect," of monsters and lethal microorganisms being created in the laboratory and escaping natural control as they enter into a defenseless environment. Differences in information and values have led to confrontation resulting in political action.

Scientists have made quantum jumps in generating knowledge of life processes and are beginning to locate in the brain sources of human behaviors and emotions. Researchers have been able to engineer microbial, plant, and animal cells to manufacture substances hitherto unavailable in quantities sufficient for practical uses in research and therapy. Advances in biology have opened the way to many new technical applications in agriculture, health, industry, and energy production. Soon protein engineering will be used to design proteins never seen in nature and processes will be developed for their manufacture by genetically engineered organisms or cells.

Commercial development is proceding at an ever-accelerating pace; over three hundred companies are now counted as bioscience-based firms[3]. Commercialization is raising issues pertaining to property rights in living material, the safety of new products, and the effect of new synthetic life forms on evolved species and ecosystems. But the most socially significant impact of advancing biotechnology appears to be in the unprecedented possibilities for managing the course of human life. Technologies are now available to affect nearly every aspect of human reproduction. Mean life expectancy is being extended with advances in knowledge and techniques in genetics, geriatrics, nutrition, and environmental health sciences, ultimately affecting population dynamics.

The major implication of the revolution in biology is that through its technological applications the human species has the option of shaping its biological future. At present that future is being shaped haphazardly by technologies now in effect or on the way, rather than by informed social choice.

It should be apparent that biotechnical advances invariably bring social, economic, legal, and ethical consequences. They induce political action that seeks to control policy and hence these issues become natural objects of study for political science. As yet, however, none of the social sciences, including political science, have acted, as disciplines, to address these issues. If humanity takes responsible control of its biological future it must, in its own interest, act in an informed and farsighted manner. Responsibility for this action must be shared among many sectors of society--notably government, learned professions, religious organizations, and philanthropic foundations. Most importantly, however, responsibility will rest with the institutions of higher education. Within the universities many disciplines relate, in principle, to some aspects of the biological revolution. On issues of policy, however, the social sciences and especially political science have the greater responsibility.

Effective public policy for guiding and safeguarding the social effects of advancing bioscience depends upon a foundation of public information and understanding that has yet to be laid down. The future course of the biological revolution and its effects will be greatly influenced by what does or does not happen to this critical development in our institutions of higher learning. Where, if not in social or political science, can this critical issue be as appropriately addressed?

III. BIOTECHNOLOGY AND SOCIAL ISSUES

The technical and intellectual revolution briefly described in the previous section has engendered political conflicts at all levels of governance, be they local, national, or international. An interesting characteristic of these conflicts is that the social sciences have been poorly represented in the attempts by society to control or resolve them. In particular, political scientists have been noticeably absent in efforts to clarify or to resolve major issues in biotechnology with obvious political implications. Examples of the types of conflicts and problems brought about by the biotechnology revolution, as well as possible conflicts of the future, are discussed in this section.

A. Social Issues Related To Time and Degree of Concern

For illustrative purposes and to provide an analytical framework, it is useful to discuss conflicts arising from biotechnology R&D and applications with reference to time frames (generalizations) and degree of societal concern (order). But it is first necessary to define these terms.

1. Time Frames

a. First generation. During the time period 1974-1978 the first of the genetic engineering techniques, rDNA, emerged. This technique allows researchers to elegantly manipulate in a purposeful manner the genetic material of animal, microbial, and plant cells. During the first generation, neither the risks nor benefits of rDNA were known. However, many practicing scientists believed the degree of risk inherent in research was low, but other scientists, less certain of the consequences of their work, gave the public a perception of risk that was significantly higher. Future benefits from rDNA research were being postulated, at times exaggerated, but only a few applications seemed feasible within a short time.

b. Second generation. This generation began about 1977, continues through the present, and may not end for another two or three years. During this time other advanced biotechnology techniques have been developed, including hybridoma construction, DNA sequencing, and protoplast fusion. Together with rDNA they can be grouped under the rubric of "genetic engineering." Sufficient information has been generated from risk assessment experiments and practical experience to allow for initial estimates of hazards associated with genetic engineering work, and they have been found vanishingly small. Practical applications are beginning to appear, particularly in health related products, and their testing and production is being done by a budding industry, termed the bioscience-based industry.

c. Third generation. In all likelihood,

the second generation will imperceptibly blend into a third. Here basic research will continue to proceed at a rapid rate, but the practical applications from earlier research will impact on ever-widening sectors of society. In particular, a mature, widely spread bioscience-based industry will become operational; "traditional" industries will adopt as required specific biotechnologies and bioprocesses. National economies will become significantly affected by the biotechnologies.

2. Degree of Concern

a. First order problem. A first order problem area has a significant actual or potential impact on world society and therefore has the attention of world leaders. It may not be contained by national boundaries. If so, its management must be sought on national and international levels. Examples include fallout from nuclear accidents, acid rain, and the AIDS pandemic.

b. Second order problem. A second order problem area has a lower order impact on, or poses conjectural hazards to, society. Nevertheless, significant sectors of society are sufficiently concerned by second order problem areas, so they remain in the public eye. Due to more pressing demands for their time and attention, high-level politicians tend to pay attention to this class of problems only if it transgresses a certain critical threshold level of public concern. Examples of second order problem areas include the increasing concentration of CO_2 in the atmosphere, the diminishing rain forests, and the destruction of the ozone layer. If fears prove to be unfounded and interest in it ebbs, a second order problem is downgraded to the third order. Of course, the converse could happen. The problem of toxic waste dumps was, until a few years ago, a second order problem; it is now of the first order.

c. Third order problem. A problem area is of the third order if it seems to pose a very low risk to society or causes small, reparable damage to the environment. Small or specialized sectors of society may focus their attention on such an area, but most of us ignore it. An example could be the growing resistance to antibiotics of some disease-causing bacterial species.

B. Political Issues Arising from Biotechnology R&D and Its Applications

Each generation of biotechnology has seen the creation of new, perhaps unique, policy issues of importance and interest to social scientists. The fact that they have been largely ignored by the social science community does not diminish their significance. For this reason, several policy issues appearing as a result of advances in biotechnology are described and their relevance to the social sciences are examined.

1. First Generation Policy Issues.

After its description in the scientific literature in 1974[4], rDNA soon became an indispensible tool to molecular biologists working in several developed countries. However, there were practitioners who worried whether the experiments being carried out or planned could pose hazards to workers and the public. In particular, a technique called "shot-gun" cloning of genes seemed fraught with danger. The fear was that, in the course of a shot-gun experiment, a possibility existed of altering a harmless microbe so that it became a virulent pathogen, perhaps one never seen before, that could escape the laboratory and wreak havoc among humans, animals, or plants.

Given this concern, the scientists who pioneered rDNA techniques acted by calling for a moratorium on their research until an international conference was held to consider whether their work was risky and, if so, what to do about it.[5] Accordingly, in 1975 molecular biologists from around the world gathered at Asilomar, California to consider the conjectural hazards posed by rDNA research. Almost as an afterthought, the organizers invited four lawyers and sixteen media representatives to attend; no social scientists were invited.

At this introductory stage of what later became known as the rDNA controversy, biotechnology posed two major sets of issues to society: how to evaluate the emerging scientific/technical area in terms of its costs and benefits to society and, based on this evaluation, how best to manage the biotechnology research, keeping in mind the possibly conflicting concepts of scientific freedom and public responsibility[6].

In considering the first issue, it was clear that one possible cost, that of hazards arising out of risky experiments, was an immediate concern. The response of the scientists at Asilomar was a prudent one. On the one hand, they decided to plan and carry out risk assessments to find out the degree of risk posed by certain types of experiments and, on the other, to draw up a list containing allowable and prohibited experiments. Those that were allowed were circumscribed by strict rules defining the containment conditions under which experiments could proceed. Although the Asilomar rules were voluntary, they were soon codified by the U.S. National Institutes of Health (NIH) and the United Kingdom's Genetic Manipulation Advisory Group. The U.S. rules, called the "NIH Guidelines," were administered by the NIH with the guidance of the newly formed Recombinant Advisory Committee (RAC)[7]. RAC was, and is, charged with adjusting the NIH Guidelines in the light of changing circumstances.

This brings us to the second set of issues. The NIH, an executive agency, promulgated the Guidelines as administrative rules, published in the Federal Register. At first, no input was sought from outside the molecular biology community. The initial makeup of RAC--only molecular biologists--reflected that situation. Soon disease experts and epidemiologists were added, then, a bit later, one social scientist and an ethicist.

Beginning in 1976, the first attempts to manage rDNA activity by legislative fiat began[8]. Eventually, uncoordinated efforts to do so were made at the municipal, state, and national levels. Only a few of the attempts at the municipal level were to succeed. However, for the first time, a limited cnumber of social scientists took part in the rDNA controversy, sometimes as members of municipal regulatory bodies, but usually as members of committees that were being set up to draft university regulations on, or position papers for, rDNA research. But when the question of federal preemption arose, where political scientists could have been the most helpful, they were absent.

As the rDNA controversy grew more heated, a spectrum of opinions about how to manage the new technology could be discerned. At one end of the spectrum were those who believed the manipulation of genes posed unimagined horrors to society and should therefore be banned; at the opposite end were the advocates of unrestricted freedom for scientists to conduct research. Of course, the situation was more complex because many shades of opinion existed between the two extremes. In the midst of the trench warfare going on between proponents of the various opinions, several members of Congress drafted bills in the late 1970s to regulate rDNA activities. An important question was whether these bills, once they became law, should preempt state and local law. If preemption was not accepted, it was possible that extremist views would find expression in local laws. Thus, the possibility existed that a national crazy quilt of municipal laws would be created, forcing molecular biologists and probably other scientists either to stop their work or to fulfill a variety of onerous conditions before they could proceed. No congressional action on regulating rDNA research was completed during the first generation; the issue continues into the second.

The rDNA controversy was a second order problem throughout the first generation, but was downgraded to the third order by the end of it. The controversy more or less died as a public issue because an ever increasing amount of experimental and empirical data, accepted by the majority of the public, indicated its safety. In particular, new and unexpected findings from research showed that genes from animals could not work in bacteria because the latter lacked certain enzymes required to assemble the information part of the animal gene. With this accumulating evidence in hand, the RAC, which as mentioned above is charged with adjusting the NIH Guidelines in the light of changing circumstances, has slowly but surely downgraded the conditions under which research can proceed. It can be seen that the Guidelines are an evolving, responsive set of rules, designed to not hinder the progress of science while adequately protecting laboratory workers and the public.

The point of the foregoing is that what began as a unique social experiment to control a potentially risky technology has turned out to be a workable model for managing technologies likely to emerge in the future. The role of political scientists in molding this control mechanism has been minimal. Further, the rDNA controversy was settled largely without any known policy contribution by political scientists.

2. Second Generation Policy Issues.

If the societal issues in the first generation can be said to have stemmed largely from uncertainties accompanying rDNA research, those in the second generation have appeared, or are likely to appear, as a result of the applications of biotechnology R&D and their equitable distribution. These issues touch on many areas encompassed within the social sciences as well as the humanities; the tendency to define issues under traditional disciplinary categories should therefore be resisted. In order to demonstrate how interdisciplinary issues are emerging from biotechnology, we discuss below seven illustrative cases to which political scientists could make major professional contributions.

a. <u>Regulation of biotechnology</u>. As of this writing, Congress has failed to pass a law regulating biotechnology. It is not for wont of trying; in early 1986, for example, three bills were introduced,[9] but none is likely to pass. Under the "Coordinated Framework for Regulation of Biotechnology," issued by the President's Office of Science and Technology Policy, several federal agencies have defined biotechnology policies and are attempting to take on responsibilities for regulating biotechnology activities that fall within their presumed spheres of responsibility. Thus, the Environmental Protection Agency (EPA) regulates the release of genetically engineered organisms into the environment (see below), the U.S. Department of Agriculture regulates animal biologic products, the Food and Drug Administration regulates drugs and diagnostics, and so forth.

In this confused but critical regulatory situation it would be useful to involve political scientists with expertise in administrative and statutory law to give an historical perspective on past management of risky science and technology and to present options for rule construction to decision makers. The question of preemption, still very much an issue, should be examined by dispassionate political scientists.

Important policy issues in the area of regulation that offer fertile research opportunities include: What would be an appropriate definition of biotechnology for regulatory purposes? What are the options for Congress in controlling biotechnology research and bioscience-based industry? Since biotechnology touches on virtually all aspects of human activity, how is its regulation to be apportioned between regulatory agencies? What are the international dimensions of rule making and their oversight?

b. The deliberate release issue. In late 1985 the California bioscience-based firm Advanced Genetic Science (AGS) received permission from the EPA to test a genetically engineered organism in the field. Shortly afterwards the multinational firm Monsanto applied for a similar permit to test a bacteria that kills insects in the soil. In the course of 1986, the first permit was revoked after AGS was found to have violated EPA test provisions, while Monsanto's application was denied, largely for political reasons. Predictably, opponents of genetic engineering research were pleased with these developments, as indeed were some proponents of biotechnology, who view field testing as warranting further examination. Reasons offered as to why field testing should not yet move forward stem from several factors: a lack of comprehensive information about the possible environmental effects of such testing; the lack of clear regulations in this area; the lack of a mechanism for monitoring the short- and long-term effects of releasing genetically engineered organisms; and the absence of Congressional action and intent in this area.

The wider-ranging policy issues revealed by the AGS and Monsanto cases that could be clarified by political scientists include: the determination of the extent to which the public should be informed of the proposed testing and how much voice it should have in the granting of testing permits; the designation of the entity that should be responsible for damages if something went wrong; the identification of international considerations for permit granting, given that the potential spread of a microorganism, either "wild" or genetically engineered, may not be deterred by international boundaries; and the designation of a public body that would be ultimately responsible for protecting the public's health in this and like situations. This listing of policy issues is not meant to assign blame; rather, its aim is to illustrate that dispassionate, objective scholarship is required to provide knowledge for both public and private enterprise decision making.

c. Genetic screening.[10] With increasingly precise probes for genetic disorders, it may become possible for the medical profession not only to diagnose at an early stage overt genetic disorders (e.g., such as rare metabolic mental impairment, sickle cell anemia, and thalassemia), but also to identify persons who carry traits for these diseases, as well as for more covert disorders such as cholesterol-associated heart disease, certain cancers, and even some forms of alcoholism. Although these advances will bring immense benefits to members of society in terms of better and earlier treatment and the development of preventive strategies for those identified as being at risk from a genetically determined disorder, possibilities for abuses exist. For example, persons identified as being at a higher than normal risk for a disorder may be discriminated against at work or by a possible employer; a carrier of a genetic

.f publicly identified, may have diffi- obtaining insurance.

A policy issue emerging from this development in biotechnology is the determination of who should have access to the sensitive information derived from genetic screening. Though results from genetic screening are protected by medical confidentiality, problems would arise if businesses required prospective employees to undergo genetic screening before employment, or if insurance companies would not issue insurance to a person before that person is genetically screened.

d. Genetic therapy/counseling. Unlike genetic screening, genetic therapy is used to treat patients suffering from genetic disorders or to prevent future disorders. At present, prevention can only be accomplished by counseling prospective parents who have been found through screening to be carrying defective genes that code for disease. In the future, genetic intervention techniques will be developed that allow medical practitioners to correct defective genes either in the cells of a specific tissue, or in the embryonic stage. If and when this happens, it might be possible to effect a cure of some genetic disorders.

The difficult situation that is arising in this area of biotechnology can be demonstrated by the social effects stemming from the discovery of diagnostic biotechniques to identify the "fragile X chromosome" in the fetus. A male inheriting this defective chromosome has a high probability of suffering a handicap that could range from being a slow learner to being severely retarded (most will fall in the latter category). Prospective parents are already faced with the decision whether to continue a pregnancy after the fetus has been identified as carrying the fragile X chromosome. In the near future, as the technique is refined, parents will have to make the agonizing decision between terminating the pregnancy and having a male child who will be, at best, only slightly retarded or a female child whose mental impairment will not be so severe, but who carries the genetic trait for the fragile X chromosome.

Besides the difficult personal decisions arising from counseling or therapy, society itself will encounter troublesome ethical and policy issues. Some of these will be affected by economic realities; for example, it may cost the community in excess of $1 million to maintain throughout life an adult with an intellectual handicap. In other countries, such as China, where strict family planning is enforced, the importance of preventing genetic disorders in the one or two permitted children may become an overriding factor. Does the right of privacy forbid a government from taking part in genetic therapy/counseling decisions? Does a government have the authority to discourage prospective parents from reproducing if both carry genes coding for a disorder? Would human rights be violated if a government prevented parents from bearing offspring likely to inherit a genetic disorder?

e. University-industry relations. Almost all basic research in the U.S. is publicly funded. Chemical and engineering departments in universities have long had to deal with issues pertaining to the ownership and use of inventions that result from their research. Similar issues are now facing life sciences departments. However, there are several characteristics peculiar to the bioscience-based industry being spawned from biotechnology R&D: (1) unlike other fields where applications from basic research take a long time to emerge, biotechnology research often comes up with findings having immediate applicability to industry and agriculture; (2) entrepreneurs of bioscience-based industry are frequently university professors; (3) there are usually close ties between bioscience firms and universities; and (4) much research leading to applications has been publicly funded. In view of these characteristics, and with the realization of commercial opportunities from research, questions have arisen about the proper relationship between universities (and their professors) and bioscience-based industries. Most universities have by this time formulated rules that govern their, and their professors', relationships with industry. However, policy issues that arose at the beginning of the time when university-industry bonds were being forged are still present; others have occurred as circumstances change.

The main issue, one that cyclically reemerges, is who, or what entity, should derive the benefits from research partially or wholly funded by the taxpayers and performed in public institutions? Several sub-issues emanate from the main issue; who has the rights to the patents of inventions developed in these institutions with public funds? Is it proper for professors/entrepreneurs to employ graduate students on industrial research projects? How much university-salaried time should a professor be allowed to spend on outside activities? To what extent may the free exchange of scientific information be curtailed in order to prevent the dissemination of knowledge of value to industry?

f. Biotechnology and the Third World.[11] It is widely recognized that biotechnology holds special promise to developing countries, for two important reasons. First, it could provide the tools to help these countries solve previously intractable problems related to health, food, and energy. Second, it may make available to these countries the means to exploit their natural resources on a sustainable level, and under environmentally sound circumstances. An added advantage is that the capital investment for biotechnology would be less than for any other advanced technology. But before most developing countries can take advantage of the promises of biotechnology, difficult social/political problems will have to be solved. Some will necessitate a government to take on very expensive obligations. These problems include the designing of policies for improving educational systems, establishing or building up the infrastructures that support and nurture science and technology, setting up mechanisms for the international transfer of biotechnology, and assisting in the forming of bioscience-based industry. The solution of these problems entails another set of issues for donor countries and organizations: should assistance be provided through bilateral links such as foreign aid, by multilateral mechanisms offered by the international organizations, by working with non-governmental organizations, or a combination of the three?

g. Biological (bacteriological) and toxin warfare.[12] One unfortunate application of biotechnology could be the design and manufacture of agents and substances for biological warfare

(BW). This misapplication of biotechnology has not been used so far because the element of control over the agent, once released, cannot be guaranteed. However, the ability to control, lacking until now, may in the future be gained through the advanced techniques of biotechnology. Further, the possibility exists for the manufacture of toxins in large quantities by genetically engineered organisms.

The policy issues that bear on this possibility include: deciding on the political steps needed to strengthen the international legal regime that checks the spread of BW; putting into effect national legislation that precludes offensive BW development; and taking steps to encourage, as confidence building measures, widespread cooperation in peaceful biotechnology R&D between scientists and research units within differing social systems. Further questions need to be answered: Is it possible to verify whether nations are abstaining from offensive BW R&D and manufacture? How can defensive (permitted) research be distinguished from offensive (banned) research? Is it possible to design and set up an international inspectorate, patterned perhaps on the International Atomic Energy Agency, to make certain that laboratories throughout the world are desisting from BW-related work?

h. Other issues. It must be stressed that the foregoing second generation policy issues are just a sampling; many other topics and issues have appeared or will do so. For example, issues not touched on in this report due to space constraints, include those pertaining to the international commerce of living organisms, intellectual property rights, the safe disposal of biowastes, government control over information, and transfer of biotechnology to hostile states.

3. Third Generation Policy Issues

The third generation will undoubtedly see a continuity of the exponential rate of growth of biotechnology R&D begun in the first generation, and of commercialization begun in the second. It may be that the number of problems generated by this tremendous activity in biotechnology will also grow exponentially. The short history of the field is not reassuring on this point; observe the growth in the number of problem areas from the first to the second generation.

It is difficult to envisage issues likely to appear in the third generation. Many will probably derive from second generation issues. For example, when it becomes possible to intervene on the genetic level for a planned purpose, perhaps to enhance a genetically determined characteristic (such as height and weight), should this be regulated? When a large number of countries develop advanced capabilities in biotechnology, would one or more of them try to develop BW as an alternative to nuclear arms? Other issues peculiar to the third generation will perhaps appear as a result of effects only measureable or observable in the long term. Yet others will come about as a result of research or applications that cannot be foreseen.

To date, political scientists have done little to grapple with the policy issues raised by biotechnology. Why this is so, and what could be done to rectify the situation, are discussed in the next sections. At this point, we simply state that it is clear that if political scientists do not familiarize themselves with public policy issues pertaining to science and technology in general, and biotechnology in particular, they will be ill-prepared to deal with problems certain to appear in biotechnology's third generation. Thus, today's overarching challenge to political scientists is: How may they contribute to the resolution of issues certain to arise during the third generation of biotechnology?

IV. STATEMENT OF THE PROBLEM

The rapid movement toward a third generation of biotechnology with its accompanying policy issues raises critical questions concerning the role of higher education in addressing them. In this section, we further develop our contention that universities are failing to assist public understanding of emerging biopolitical issues. Second and third generation issues in applied biology raise problems for social policy and personal conduct, the solutions to which involve the basic purposes of liberal arts education. Until these problems are forthrightly addressed, universities are derelict in their responsibility to prepare students for responsible citizenship in a world being rapidly changed by the biosciences. Despite the need for attention to public policy for biotechnology, few universities even offer courses relating to this topic. Only a few provide their students with opportunities for exposure to biology-related issues or offer curricula in science, technology, and public policy. Although the movement of many universities back toward a core curriculum concept offers, in theory, an excellent opportunity to generate creative, innovative, interdisciplinary curricula, in practice this option has seldom been taken. Instead, universities have opted simply to require students to select from a list of science courses organized along inflexible disciplinary lines that do not reflect the dynamic interaction of the humanistic, biological, and social aspects of current and future problems. They not only fail to prepare students to understand science-related social issues, they also tend to discourage efforts of faculty members who receive few institutional rewards for interdisciplinary initiatives and who often must pursue interdisciplinary teaching interests on an overload basis, if they are approved at all.

Higher education's neglect of the awesome issues of the biological revolution will result in the passing on to society of graduates ill-prepared to deal with many critical problems of the real world. Students are not well educated in science-based issues that affect them personally both today and as tomorrow's responsible citizens and leaders. The unresponsiveness of higher education cuts both ways. Those being trained in science are not systematically receiving a sensitizing to the broader social implications of their future work. Likewise, students in the liberal arts and professions have little appreciation of the sciences and are unaware of the powerful impact that science and technology have on their lives. This may in part be attributed to the lack of a meaningful interdisciplinary framework for their studies and in part because of an aversion to science as usually taught.

In addition to the lack of an interdisciplinary curriculum for addressing biotechnology issues, undergraduate liberal arts instruction tends to ignore important contributions to knowledge by biologists and the critical insights biology can provide for the study of the human experience. Professors in the humanities and social sciences seldom have backgrounds in the physical or biological sciences sufficient for an appreciation of the relevance of those sciences to social and political issues. As a consequence, when degree requirements and curricula are adopted, little, if any, recognition is given to the implications of science in general or biology in particular.

Ironically, many educators who argue the importance of classical political thought often discount the relevance of contemporary thinking by biologists, some of whom have written persuasively on the need to understand science-related social and ethical issues. These academic conservatives are often among the more vocal critics in departments when innovative courses are proposed. Perhaps they should take a more perceptive and critical-minded view of the past, recalling the classical thinkers who recognized the linkage between biology and society and used biological models to elucidate politics. Even though Aristotle's and Plato's concepts of biology were wrong, their insights on societies and governments remain relevant. They would probably be among the first to recognize the importance of the issues now brought forth by biotechnology, issues raising fundamental questions regarding ethics and values in human behavior. These questions, basic to political thought, include the evaluation of human life, the uniqueness of human existence vis-a-vis other species, the characteristics of human nature, and the biological "rights" of humans. All are inseparable from the new biotechnology. Moreover, few technologies more sharply pose dilemmas concerning individual rights versus social needs than do present day advances in biology and medicine. These dilemmas relate to which freedoms are to be preferred when freedoms conflict, to the extent to which society ought to intervene in these conflicts, and the rational and moral justification of asserted rights. For instance, is the right to reproduce inalienable and if it is, what does that mean in light of advances in biotechnology and the life sciences generally? More specific to academia are questions concerning the "right" to perform unhindered scientific research. The issues raised by biotechnological developments touch on every student as a member of society and a future participant in the shaping of social policy.

Although higher education and liberal arts share the responsibility for educating students on these issues, political science bears a heavy responsibility because of its special focus on social policy. If political science is to retain its role in contributing toward an understanding of public policy, it must broaden its scope of attention commensurate with the scope of society-wide issues.

As a discipline, political science has become intellectually isolated with respect to issues in science and technology in general and in biology and medicine in particular. Whereas medical sociology, medical history, medical anthropology, and medical ethics are firmly established subfields of their disciplines with an accompanying influence on the study of medicine, a focused area of biopolicy in political science is conspicuously absent. This absence is all the more glaring if political science is regarded as the lead discipline in the study of public policy. Although some individual political scientists have begun to deal with biopolicy issues, the efforts to date have been isolated, fragmented, and little recognized by the discipline. Because of the rejection of science and technology policy studies by many political science departments, some concerned faculty have moved out of their departments and established autonomous science policy programs elsewhere in their universities, or joined ongoing programs in science, technology, and society.

Not surprisingly, government commissions, panels, and other agencies making decisions in biotechnology rarely include representatives from political science. To a large extent, this reflects the lack of interest and of influence on the part of political scientists or, more seriously, a feeling within these policy-making bodies that political scientists have little to offer. For political science to have a voice in the decision process, evidence of informed concern and relevant analytic capabilities is necessary. With or without the input of political scientists, however, biotechnology policy will be made. Unfortunately, policies have been too often adopted without an adequate assessment of political implications that participation by political scientists could have provided. A consequence has been ineffective or contentious policy implementation.

Initiatives for studying the policy implications of biotechnology have, to date, come from outside political science. For instance, the Hastings Center with its widely read Report is the product of persons trained in bioethics, even though much of its work is squarely in the arena of public policy. Journals in bioethics have a heavy policy emphasis despite the absence of political scientists. Similarly, a major policy-oriented journal, Issues in Science and Technology, did not originate from political science. Instead, it was launched by physical and biological scientists through the National Academy of Sciences, the National Academy of Engineering, and the Institute of Medicine.

A few political scientists have been critical of the work of some natural scientists writing on policy issues and who appear to lack appreciation of the intricacies of the policy process. Even if these critiques are accurate, the primary criticism ought to be directed not at the scientists who, by default, are leading the policy dialogue, but more logically at the defaultees, those explicitly trained to deal with public policy--the political scientists.

V. ADDRESSING THE PROBLEM

The academic problem is multifaceted and the issues with which it is concerned affect not only different levels of society, but also different entities within levels. In order to assist society in addressing biopolitical issues the universities must first redress their failure to provide an effective response to implications of an advancing biotechnology. This section will examine how political science and biology departments, university administrators, private foundations, and government can cooperate to create the educational means needed to consider public policy issues relating to biotechnology. We begin with political science.

A. The Role of Political Science Departments

Central to any activity in this area is the reorientation of departments of political science to a more open posture with regard to appropriate subject matter for political scientists. Given the intellectual revolution initiated by twentieth century biologists and the very basic policy questions emerging from that work, political scientists can no longer afford to disregard the findings, concepts, and implications emerging from the new biotechnology. Perhaps the change most needed in the discipline is recognition within political science departments that, if they are to retain their vitality, their scope and content are going to be reshaped either from within or altered by irresistable forces from without. Once this is understood, the process of incorporating new knowledge from the life sciences and employing individuals who want to work with that knowledge will become much easier.

Although these comments may seem innocuous, they have far-reaching implications. Many political scientists believe that the life sciences lie outside the bounds of political science interests. This strikes us as injudicious, reflecting an ideological bias rather than a considered judgment. When this barrier of intellectual exclusiveness is removed, departments of political science will become more accepting of faculty members with a biological orientation. Political scientists working in biology and biotechnology related areas can then seek tenure and promotion wihout fear of being stigmatized as having departed from the discipline. Indeed, the introduction of biologically oriented faculty into departments of political science should "energize" those departments to rethink their missions in the contemporary world of scholarship.

It should be noted that political science has not always been hesitant to break new ground, particularly in its relationship to biology. In fact, there seems to have been a progressive narrowing of the field since its formative period in the earlier decades of this century. A reading of the presidential addresses and articles of the "founders" of the American Political Science Association demonstrates a clear interest in the interdisciplinary goals of the discipline, especially as it related to biology and psychology. The following quotations illustrate this early concern. In 1921, Charles E. Merriam stated:

> From time to time the study of politics has been completely abreast with current science of the time, as in the days of Aristotle, and from time to time has drifted away again in scholasticism and legalism of the narrowest type. . .In our day the cross fertilization of politics with science, so called, or more strictly with modern methods of inquiry and investigation might not be unprofitable.[13]

William Bennett Munro, in his 1927 presidential address to the American Political Science Association, argued that

> Our immediate goal, therefore, should be to release political science from the old metaphysical and juristic concepts upon which it has traditionally been based ...

> It is to the natural sciences that we may most profitably turn, in this hour of transition, for suggestions as to the reconstruction of our postulates and methods[14] (Emphasis added).

Perhaps the clearest statement of the special reciprocal relationship between the natural sciences and the social sciences comes from Charles Merriam in his 1925 APSA presidential address[15]:

> The essential consideration is that the point of view and the contacts are obtained and sustained in the various fields of social inquiry; that twilight zones are not allowed to lie neglected; that partial treatment does not twist and warp the judgment of social observers and analysts . . .
>
> Still more serious for the student of politics is the integration of social science with the results of what is called natural science--the reunion of the natural and the "non-natural" sciences. For more and more it appears that the last word in human behavior is to be scientific; more and more clearly it becomes evident that the social and political implications of natural science are of fundamental importance. It even seems at times that this is more evident to the natural scientists than to the social scientists, who at times concede the impossibility of more scientific social control of human conduct.
>
> Biology, psychology, anthropology, psychopathology, medicine, the earth sci-

> ences, are now reaching out to consider the application of their conclusions to social situations. . . What shall be the attitude of politics and social sciences to these new developments and these new challenges? Shall we hold them in contempt of court, these irreverent natural scientists, or shall we ostracize them till they submit to our laws; or shall we outvote them; or shall we merely ignore them, and go our way?. . .<u>If they are to govern the world they must and doubtless will learn more of politics and social relations. Perhaps they are more impressed with the significance of the social implications of natural science than we are</u> (Emphasis added).

Little can be added today to strengthen what Merriam said. Within the context of the emerging biotechnological revolution, Merriam's ob servations are as relevant now as they were sixty years ago, and as they also were to Harold Lasswell.[16] The opportunities that Merriam foresaw for political scientists have increased dramatically and so have the penalties for failure to respond.

There are, however, indications of responsive change; opinion in the the organizational headquarters of the American Political Science Association is quite supportive of creative, innovative, and cross-disciplinary initiatives in biotechnology policy. Partly in response to the movement of creative scholars away from the discipline, APSA has authorized the establishment of an official section devoted to politics and the life sciences and a section on science and technology studies in response to growing professional interest.

What we are chiefly missing today is encouragement from the academic practitioners of the discipline and from the departments who, by their hiring practices and course offerings, shape the discipline and provide incentives and disincentives for certain types of research and teaching. In the end, leadership in shaping the future course of political science will most likely come from those departments that encourage future-oriented faculty members to do innovative, interdisciplinary work.

Departments having faculties with an interest in the life sciences will be in a position to lend their professional expertise to citizens, scholars, lawmakers, and other government officials in the current quest for knowledge about the policy implications of biotechnology. Such expertise will project political scientists into a challenging set of contemporary intellectual developments. Certainly the discipline would hardly be disadvantaged by being perceived as relevant to a major problem area of the late twentieth century. Recent preoccupation with methodology to the neglect of content has created an image of an irrelevant political science in the minds of many students. Let us now turn to ways in which undergraduate and graduate curricula may address the problem.

1. Undergraduate Curricular Revisions.

New undergraduate courses are needed to reflect the changed intellectual environment brought about by the biological revolution. As a recent editorial in the journal *Perspectives in Biology and Medicine* observed, "we. . . see the 'New Biology' as worthy of attention in its own right for the powerful role it will come

to play in the thinking of all educa
zens. . ."[17] Because modern society
understanding of life and social behavi
been so strongly shaped by scientists as in
ential as Bernard, Darwin, Mendel, Watson, a
Crick, surely we must incorporate a consideration of their works alongside those of traditional political philosophy. Although each university will shape its curriculum in its own way, we believe that a contemporary general education curriculum must include courses linking the humanities and the social sciences with biology and biotechnology. In many instances this could be done in general courses in science, technology, and society. Not only will this broaden the intellectual horizon of students, it will also contribute to breaking down artificial barriers between disciplines and between individual faculty members.

In addition, courses must be developed for undergraduate political science majors as part of their bachelor's degree preparation. At the very least, a survey course in science, technology, and society that includes the range of issues in which biology and biotechnology impact upon political behavior and public policy ought to be required. Where feasible, more specialized undergraduate courses can be developed. With a proper introduction to this subject matter at the undergraduate level, some students will be encouraged to pursue biologically relevant course work in their graduate studies.

2. Graduate Curricular Revisions.

Important as undergraduate studies are, the major societal need is for advanced interdisciplinary specialists who can work at the juncture he life sciences and the social sciences. The most pressing need is for political scientists who can analyze complex issues arising out of the rapidly expanding knowledge base in biotechnology. The training of such specialists requires significant revisions in the traditional structure of political science departments and in expectations regarding the capabilities of their graduates.

Individual departments will, of course, revise their curricula in ways that are consistent with local faculty resources, institutional structure, academic clientele, and funding opportunities. Some departments will create a new subfield, others may incorporate biopolicy studies into already existing science policy or environmental studies programs, and still others might integrate biopolicy into general public policy analysis undertakings. Precisely how this is done is not as important as the real opening up of graduate training in this area.

In addition to a solid foundation of empirical skills in policy analysis, students need opportunities for instruction in governmental science policy making, risk assessment, national and international issues in biotechnology, biological influences on political value systems, biobehavioral political theory, and bioethics. Education in these areas, in combination with traditional course work in political science, will prepare students for the developing vocational opportunities of the 1990s and beyond. The discipline of political science should not relinquish its opportunity for incorporating new intellectual realities within its field of interest. Students emerging from M.A. and Ph.D. programs should be prepared for the world which awaits _them_, rather than for the world in which their professors were educated years previously.

Beyond the need for specialists in the public policy aspects of biotechnology to teach and conduct research in universities, there are numerous placement opportunities outside of higher education. These exist in private sector public policy research institutes, in federal and state science policy research centers, on staffs of legislative committees engaged in science-based lawmaking, and in regulatory agencies that deal with public policy questions emerging from basic life science research and innovation in biotechnology. Beyond these are medical school research units, which are increasingly seeking out social scientists to work on biomedical policy questions, and the biotechnology industry, which has a major stake in regulatory issues related to research and commercial applications.

As the biological revolution accelerates, the public policy agenda is becoming increasingly infused with biologically and biotechnologically based issues. As a result, the demand for interdisciplinary policy analysts will increase dramatically in the years ahead. If the discipline of political science ignores this reality, it does so at its own peril, because it will have surrendered the opportunity to have a relevant and important voice in what has been called the dominant intellectual thrust of the twenty-first century.

B. Links with Biologists

Biologists have an important role to play in fostering within political science a sensitivity to the public policy dimensions of biotechnology. Political scientists and biologists can develop mutually rewarding relationships. For example, biologists can serve as informal consultants to biologically oriented political scientists; political science faculty can conduct seminars and workshops regarding political issues in the life sciences. Also, these relationships can extend to mutual services for government and the private sector.

These relationships will vary depending upon the individuals involved and type of programming undertaken. The key element to be stressed here, however, is that the relationship should be mutually respectful rather than adversarial. On the one hand, political scientists must realize that biologists do not normally receive disciplinary rewards for engaging in public policy research. Biologists have a tendency to discount this type of intellectual endeavor unless forced to become involved, as was the case during the initial rDNA controversy. On the other hand, biologists must recognize the study of public policy questions as legitimate activity for political scientists. Those policy analysts who turn their attention to the life science arena need help and encouragement, not condescension. Indeed, as a repository of relevant expertise is developed, the work of political scientists should become increasingly useful, for example, in committees on biohazards, bioethics, and human subjects review.

Beyond the faculty level, interdisciplinary undergraduate and graduate student contacts should be facilitated. Although these interrelationships are beyond the scope of this report, certainly cross-disciplinary course work should have a high priority. In some instances, courses could be cross listed. In addition to the knowledge transferred, a mutual intellectual comprehension and appreciation could be expected to emerge.

C. Role of University Administrators

By its very nature, academic innovation requires wise and creative administrators beyond the department, especially at the college level. This is the case because innovation within a department often threatens well-established departmental interests. Creative initiatives are not always welcomed within departments. Furthermore, innovation can require that departments surrender resources in one subfield in order to undertake a new initiative. The perceptive college dean will understand the dynamics of this type of situation and know how to deal with it constructively in the interests of the students and the institution.

The dean has a special role to play with regard to interdisciplinary programming. The vested interests of individual disciplines are often difficult to overcome. It is the dean who has the authority to require disciplines to "talk" to each other; and it is the dean who decides the allocation of financial resources. Because no individual department sees interdisciplinary initiatives as its primary responsibility or highest priority, the dean must protect and nurture those initiatives to implementation. A difficulty to overcome is that university decision-making committees are usually structured to deal with departments representing single discipline interests, thus resulting in a situation in which interdisciplinary initiatives lack fully committed patrons. These reflections underscore the fact that, without a dean willing to commit administrative resources toward developing creative interdisciplinary initiatives, there appears little chance of their success.

For interdisciplinary initiatives to succeed at the university level, presidents, vice presidents for academic affairs, and graduate deans must foster a spirit of innovation on their campuses; and this means more than rhetorical support. If departments are disadvantaged by attempting innovative programs there will be little innovation. High level administrators could set aside venture capital which colleges can use either to study program feasibility or to implement approved programs. Moreover, administrators must be willing to support creative undertakings through lean years to mature development. More than "seed money" is usually required.

For research and instructional programs in public policies relating to biotechnology, support beyond the department level appears critical. Departments of political science that are serious in this endeavor will have recognized that their innovative initiatives require maneuvering through the bureaucratic complexities of academic institutions. Sympathetic administrators, for their part, must be sensitive to the peculiar difficulties of interdisciplinary programming and must assist departments through this complex innovative process.

D. Role of Private Foundations

Philanthropic organizations have a vital

role to play in the implementation of public policy programs in biotechnology. This will be a major undertaking, on the order of the effort and resources that were devoted to stimulating public awareness of, and academic interest in, environmental issues some twenty years ago. Many foundations may need to rethink their mission statements if they intend to show an interest in the study of public policy for biotechnology, and to allocate resources into stimulating the growth of work in this vital area. Of course, for this to happen foundations must overcome their preference for restricting their funding to "mainstream" activities, e.g., those currently in vogue in academia. They should not be fearful of being in the forefront of a new area of concern.

Foundations could provide a valuable service in support for curriculum development, for graduate fellowships, for research, and in some instances for publication. Departments of political science are already years behind in implementing curricula to train policy analysts in biotechnology. Indeed, as we have described above, virtually nothing has been done. In making funds available for curriculum development, foundations can have a major generative effect in this area that might also benefit other areas of their concerns, for example in agriculture, health, and many social issues.

Support for students is also vital. The dilemma here is that students have a natural reluctance to risk entering an emerging intellectual area without a guarantee of financial support. If fellowship funds were available, students would be encouraged to enter public policy programs in biotechnology and, moreover, their movement through those programs to completion of the Ph.D. degree would be accelerated.

Although we consider the development of instructional programs to be the highest priority for philanthropic organizations, consideration should also be given to support for research. Again, so little public policy scholarship has been produced by political scientists in the area of biotechnology, that any stimulative investment here is likely to have far-reaching payoffs in addressing policy issues in biotechnology. Foundations might also assist public outreach programs of universities on biotechnology issues. Joint sponsorship of, or funding for, conferences and workshops could hasten the growth of a biologically literate public that is able to bring informed and rational participation to the consideration of biology-related issues.

Private biotechnology firms and trade associations, although not formally classified as philanthropic organizations, should provide some support for curriculum development, students, and research. Both of these groups have a major interest in the regulatory questions relating to biotechnology; and they will become employers of some of the policy analysts trained in the universities. Thus, in their own interest, assistance from them ought to be expected.

E. Role of Government

Government has a special responsibility to stimulate the development of public policy programs in biotechnology. Much of the life-science research in post-World War II resulted in an explosion of biological knowledge and its application in biotechnology, and continues to be funded by the federal government. Indeed, if the federal government had not funded research in this area, there might not be the necessity to construct and examine public policies related to the social implications of biotechnology.

While the federal government should lend its support to objectives similar to those that we expect from foundations, it should also consider establishment of several major research centers devoted primarily to the study of public policy and the life sciences. Because the unfolding of capabilities in biotechnology promises to be a continuous process, the long-term justification for analytic studies is already established. Academic response to policy problems is already very late. In December 1986 a subcommittee of the House of Representatives Committee on Science and Technology released a report and recommendations anticipating a coordinative legal framework for regulating biotechnical innovatives from research to release.[18]

In light of a shift of social responsibilities from the federal to the state level underway for the past half decade, it seems probable that significant responsibilities for programmatic development in this area will be carried by state governments. This will involve not only the executive and legislative branches of government, but also governing boards in higher education. As science-based issues get "pushed down" to the state level, expertise will be needed to deal with them. Before enacting laws, legislatures will require considerable information on new biotechnologies and their implications. Specialists will be employed on the staffs of legislative committees as well as in science policy research units that serve state governments. Moreover, because some issues in biotechnology, such as containment procedures and questions of the release of novel microorganisms, can involve local communities, a need may develop for local or regional expertise in regulatory aspects of biotechnology. Given this situation, states have a major role to play in generating a flow of trained specialists who can conduct sophisticated policy analyses in a life science context. As a result, state officials, governing boards, universities, and departments of political science will mutually benefit from cooperative engagement in developing both public policies and academic programs that will serve critical public interests.

VI. CONCLUSION

The involvement of social scientists during the first generation of biotechnology was minimal. In fact, the rDNA controversy, during which a number of contentious public policy issues were raised, was settled without help from political scientists. But, as mentioned in the body of this report, the participation of the political science community could have had several beneficial effects: It might have led to better rule making; the degree of acceptance by the public of the NIH Guidelines could have been improved; and, as a result, the public's suspicions about genetic engineering could have been to some extent mitigated.

Now again a rise in public concern is apparent, this time about how applications from biotechnology are being tested. Are tests be[illegible] carried out in a safe manner and are they being adequately controlled and monitored by regulatory agencies? Dubious practices by isolated bioscience firms, inept regulatory procedures, and/or inept application of those procedures have played into the hands of activists who condemn all genetic engineering research and seek to stop it using whatever legal and political tactics are available. Demogogic strategies rarely serve the public interest; therefore, the involvement of political scientists is, more than ever, a necessity, if rationality is to be brought to the public debate. Through their involvement, major benefits will likely accrue to social and political science and to wider communities inside and outside of the universities.

Not only could a social and political science involvement help to counteract unconstuctive and distorting attacks on biotechnology, there would be widely shared benefits from informed, national approaches to biopolicy. First, science would benefit. Although it is commonly accepted now that the NIH Guidelines are an appropriate response to manage rDNA research, a more inclusive set of principles is needed to manage ever-expanding research and its applications. It is most important that public distrust of scientists and science does not grow to the extent of hindering beneficial research. If biotechnology were placed in a regulatory straightjacket, American preeminence in science would be diminished, technological progress would slow, and education and the economy would be retarded. The best way to prevent these unfavorable possibilities would be to develop a regulatory regime that balances the right of

o proceed with research and the
e public to know about it and, most
ly, to make informed judgments regard-
benefits and risks.

Second, the public could benefit in two ways. Over time it would benefit through the growth of a more informed and interested citizenry, and through development of enlightened university curricula that provided rational assessment of the implications of biotechnology. More immediately, an educated citizenry is essential to ensure that elected officials are aware of and act upon the interests of the broader public when they undertake to regulate biotechnology.

Third, social science would benefit. It has become almost axiomatic that the significant advances in science take place at the interstices between disciplines: i.e., the most creative work is of an interdisciplinary nature. Certainly the stunning advances in biotechnology have occurred as a result of interactions between molecular biologists, geneticists, microbiologists, biochemists, and bioengineers. Corroborative evidence can be readily found by noting the interdisciplinary orientations of recent recipients of Nobel prizes in the sciences and economics. There is reason to believe that equally fruitful collaboration on policy issues could be had if political scientists adopted a more interdisciplinary interest in science and technology in general, and biotechnology in particular. As we have indicated in this report, many advances in biotechnology have wide-ranging social and political impacts, and thus demand interdisciplinary attention. The cross-fertilization between the study of politics and the natural sciences, as the early pioneers of political science suggested, could well lead to major intellectual breakthroughs.

Thus, a challenge confronts the profession of political science. Will it be constructively engaged with the critical issues of the intellectual and technological revolution in the life sciences or will it stand aside, showing little interest in the political implications of advancing biotechnology while the mainstream of creativity in the study of social policy flows through other channels? The preponderance of emerging biopolitical issues assures that they will somehow be addressed. People and their governments will use the means available to resolve compelling issues of social policy engendered by advances in the life sciences. If the means are not available in the universities or through interdisciplinary leadership in social and political science, means will be found elsewhere. The decline of present social science disciplines and their replacement by new configurations of learning is a possibility illustrated by the history of universities.

We rest our case for attention to the social implications of advances in the life sciences and biotechnology by concluding with what may be the strongest argument of all. This is the need for prevision in guiding the course of these life-shaping sciences and in finding valid criteria for wisdom in responsive social action. Foresight and conjecture are indispensible attributes of good policy and, as Bertrand de Jouvenal pointed out years ago, they are also innate attributes of political science.[19] Prediction is more art than science, yet it is employed daily in the conduct of public affairs.

The power latent in the new biotechnology places a high premium on obtaining the best available prognosis of its effects. Best guesses are better than poor ones and require that all identifiable implications of potentially powerful innovations be considered. This analysis will inevitably include social impacts and their likely political consequences. Now more than ever political science is called upon to perform its historical role of anticipating possible futures and pointing the ways to attain or avoid them. Without involvement in the biological revolution it will no longer be able to fulfill what may be its greatest social utility.

VII. GLOSSARY

Amino acid: The chief chemical components of proteins.

Biotechnology: The collection of industrial processes that involve the use of biological systems. Processes could include the use of genetically engineered microorganisms or cells.

Chromosomes: The thread-like nuclear components of a cell that contain the hereditary material of the organism. They are composed of DNA and protein and contain most of the cell's DNA.

Clone: A group of genetically identical cells or organisms that asexually descended from a common ancestor. All cells in the clone have the same genetic material and are exact copies of the original.

DNA (deoxyribonucleic acid): The genetic material found in all living organisms. Every inherited characteristic has its origin somewhere in the code of an individual's complement of DNA.

DNA sequencing: A biochemical process that allows strips of DNA to be read as a sequence of nucleotides, permitting a translation of the genetic code into a predicted sequence of amino acids in a protein. This technique allows, for example, for the construction of new proteins and the detection of defective mutations in a gene.

Gene: The hereditary unit; a segment of DNA that codes for a specific protein.

Genetic engineering: A general heading for techniques, such as recombinant DNA and protoplast fusion, that may be used at the laboratory level to alter the hereditary apparatus of a living cell so that the cell can produce more or different chemicals, or perform completely new functions. Some altered cells may see use in industrial production.

Hybridoma: A hybrid cell, produced by the fusion of a tumor cell with an antibody-producing cell, which can be grown in tissue culture to produce highly specific antibodies (monoclonal antibodies).

Nucleotide: The basic structural unit of DNA.

Protoplast fusion: A means for achieving genetic transformation by joining two protoplasts (cells without walls) or joining a protoplast with any of the components of another cell.

Recombinant DNA (rDNA): The hybrid DNA produced by joining in the laboratory, through the use of enzymes, pieces of DNA from different sources.

Shot gun cloning: A method where by a researcher uses one or more enzymes to fragment all the genetic material in a cell. Each fragment can then be amplified by cloning for further study.

Toxin: A proteinaceous metabolic byproduct produced by a microorganism that elicits a toxic reaction on introduction in animal tissue.

VIII. END NOTES

1. D.Fleming,"On Living in a Biological Revolution," The Atlantic Monthly 223(2): 64-70 (1969).

2. U.S. Office of Technology Assessment, Impacts of Applied Genetics (Washington, D.C.: Office of Technology Assessment, 1981).

3. U.S. Office of Technology Assessment, Commercial Biotechnology: An International Analysis (Washington,D.C.: Office of Technology Assessment, 1984).

4. S. N. Cohen, "The Manipulation of Genes," Scientific American 233(1): 24-33 (1975).

5. P.Berg,et al., "Potential Biohazards of Recombinant DNA Molecules," Science 185: 303 (1974).

6. S. Krimsky, Genetic Alchemy: A Social History of the Recombinant DNA Controversy (Cambridge: MIT Press, 1983).

7. D. S. Fredrickson, "A History of the Recombinant DNA Guidelines in the United States," in _Recombinant DNA and Genetic Experimentation_, J. Morgan and W. J. Whelan, eds. (Oxford and New York: Pergamon Press, 1979), 151-6.

8. B.K. Zimmerman, "Science and Politics: DNA Comes to Washington," in _The Gene Splicing Wars: Relections on the Recombinant DNA Controversy_, R. A. Zilinskas and B. K. Zimmerman, eds. (New York: Macmillan Publishing Company, 1986), 33-53.

9. H.R. 4452, H.R. 5271, and S.R. 1967.

10. U.S.Office of Technology Assessment, _Genetic Screening in the Workplace_ (Washington, D.C.: Office of Technology Assessment, 1983).

11. U.S. National Research Council, _Priorities in Biotechnology Research for International Development_ (Washington, D. C.: National Academy Press, 1982).

12. S. Wright and R. L. Sinsheimer, "Recombinant DNA and Biological Warfare," _Bulletin of the Atomic Scientists_ 39: 20-6 (1983); E. Geissler, ed., _Biological and Toxin Weapons Today_ (London and New York: Oxford University Press, 1986); and R. A. Zilinskas, "Recombinant DNA Research and Biological Warfare," in Zilinskas and Zimmerman _Gene Splicing Wars_, 167-203.

13. C. E. Merriam, "The Present State of the Study of Politics," _American Political Science Review_ 15: 173-91 (1921).

14. W. B. Munro, "Physics and Politics--An Old Analogy Revised," American Political Science Review 22: 1-11 (1928).

15. C.E. Merriam, "Progress in Political Research," American Political Science Review 22: 1-17 (1926).

16. H. Lasswell, "The Study of the Ill as a Method of Research into Political Personalities," American Political Science Review 23: 996-1001 (1929).

17. Editorial, "A New Perspective for Biology: Its Central Role in the Liberal Arts Education of the Future," Perspectives in Biology and Medicine 29(4): 489-92 (1986).

18. House Committee on Science and Technology, Subcommittee on Investigation and Oversight, Issues in the Federal Regulation of Biotechnology: From Research to Release. 99th Cong., 2d sess., December 1986, Committee Print.

19. B. de Jouvenal, "Political Science and Prevision," American Political Science Review 59(1): 29-38 (1965).

IX. BIOGRAPHICAL STATEMENTS

Robert H. Blank is Professor of Political Science at Northern Illinois University. Previously, he was Professor and Chairman of the Political Science Department at the University of Idaho. He has held Fulbright Lectureships in Taiwan and New Zealand, where he taught and consulted on biomedical policy. His research interests are primarily in biomedical policy, particularly in the area of human genetics and reproduction. Among his publications are *The Political Implications of Human Genetic Technology*, *Redefining Human Life: Reproductive Technologies and Social Policy*, and a forthcoming book on *Rationing Medicine*.

Lynton K. Caldwell is Bentley Professor of Political Science Emeritus and Professor of Public and Environmental Affairs at Indiana University. He is the author of more than two hundred scholarly articles and seven books, his most recent being *Biocracy: Public Policy and the Life Sciences*.

Scientific and governmental bodies with which he has been associated include, among others, the Congressional Research Service, the National Research Council, the United States Senate, the National Institutes of Health, the Office of Technology Assessment, and the National Commission on Materials Policy. His 1964 article, "Biopolitics: Science, Ethics and Public Policy," has been widely credited with initiating academic interest in the political implications of the "biological revolution."

Thomas C. Wiegele is Professor of Political Science and Director, Program for Biosocial Research at Northern Illinois University. He also serves as editor of the journal Politics and the Life Sciences and as executive director of the Association for Politics and the Life Sciences. Professor Wiegele has long been interested in the impact of biology on the social sciences and two of his books, Biopolitics: Search for a More Human Political Science and Biology and the Social Sciences: An Emerging Revolution, deal with this topic.

Raymond A. Zilinskas was a clinical microbiologist before earning his doctorate in International Relations. He then worked as an analyst for the U.S. Office of Technology Assessment on its project Commercial Biotechnology: An International Analysis; as an industrial development officer for the United Nations Industrial Development Organization (UNIDO) in its Advanced Technologies Branch; and is now a consultant on science policy in Santa Monica, California serving organizations such as the Rand Corporation, the United Nations University, and UNIDO. He is the co-editor of the book The Gene Splicing Wars: Reflections on the Recombinant DNA Controversy.